GOD'S TIME FOR MANKIND

Reflections on the Church Year

GOD'S TIME FOR MANKIND

Reflections on the Church Year

by
WALTER KASPER

translated by John Griffiths

FRANCISCAN HERALD PRESS
1434 WEST 51st STREET ● CHICAGO, 60609

First published in German as GOTTES ZEIT FÜR MENSCHEN in 1978 by Verlag Herder of Freiburg in Breisgau, Federal Republic of Germany.

Copyright © Verlag Herder Freiburg im Breisgau 1978. This translation copyright © Franciscan Herald Press 1984. Translated by John Griffiths. All rights reserved.

Library of Congress Cataloging in Publication Data:

Kasper, Walter.
   God's time for mankind.
   Translation of Gottes Zeit für Menschen.
   1. Church year sermons. 2. Catholic Church —
Sermons. 3. Sermons, German — Translations into
English. 4. Sermons, English — Translations from
German. I. Title.
BX1756.K35G6713   252'.6   80-19949
ISBN 0-8199-0812-6

Published with Ecclesiastical Approval

Made in the United States of America

Contents

Preface 7

I
Mary: Model of Faith 9
Advent: Luke 1:39–47

II
The Humanity and Spirituality of Christian Joy 17
Advent: Philippians 4:4–9

III
The Word is made Flesh 27
Christmas: John 1:14

IV
Repentance as the Way to Christian Freedom 35
Lenten Penance: Mark 1:14–15

V
"Do this in memory of me" 43
Maundy Thursday: I Corinthians 11:23–26

VI
"He saw and believed" 47
Easter Sunday: John 20:1–9

VII
On the Road to Emmaus 53
Easter Monday: Luke 24:13–35

VIII
Experience of the Spirit 59
Pentecost: Romans 8:19–30

IX
Bread for the Life of the World 69
Corpus Christi: Luke 9:10–17

Preface

This book consists of sermons that I have given over the last two years in various parishes. The attempt to combine responsible academic theology with normal preaching has increasingly become a personal concern and a constantly inspiring task over the years. However exact, a distinction must be made between theology and prolamation; both can remain vital only if they are interrelated to their mutual benefit. Each in its own way seeks to approach the same goal: that of asserting God's presence in human time.

Tübingen, June 1978   WALTER KASPER

1
Mary: Model of Faith
Advent: Luke 1:39-47

AT THIS TIME we are occupied with various preparations for, and thoughts about, the approaching feast of Christmas. For the most part they have to do with the external framework of our celebration. But have we also thought about the inner meaning of Christmas? With the text mentioned above from Luke's Gospel the Church invites us to make that kind of pre-Christmas reflection, and it places the figure of Mary at the midpoint of our thinking. For Mary almost uniquely defines what we are about at this time.

The decisive statement in the text referred to is: "Blessed is she who believed." Mary is presented here as the primary model of Christian faith and as the model of the Church, the community of the faithful. Through Mary we obtain something like a picture of what faith means and of what is promised to us through faith.

1. Model of decision in faith

The courage and tenacity of faith were necessary in order

to follow the way that Mary took. As a young girl who grew up in a small, poor and obscure village she risks a venture that no woman before her has ever had to undertake. She is to become the mother of the awaited and hoped-for Messiah, the Son of God. How her task is to be performed is something she knows nothing about whatsoever. For her as for us it is a divine mystery, a miracle of God's love. But Mary dares to take God's road; a road that is so very different to that taken by other girls then as now; a road that must involve her in severe misunderstandings even with Joseph, her betrothed. Mary has the courage to be different and to do something extraordinary. She is in the best possible sense an emancipated young woman who dares to question the average set of standards and to ground her life on the quite different standards of God. Mary believes. That means that she builds wholly and solely on God for whom "everything is possible." She says Yes. "Behold, I am the handmaid of the Lord." In this way she makes herself entirely available to God and entirely available to others.

With her decision of faith Mary puts herself in a long line of great Israelite women: Sarah, Rachel, Anna, Esther, and Judith. All of them saw faith as more than an outward profession of belief. For them it was much more — an all-inclusive direction of their lives. It was always the unfruitful, the weak, who, trusting in God, obtained the strength to offer their people new life and new hope. In the Magnificat, Mary summarizes this transvaluation of the usual world-order: "He has put down the mighty from their thrones, and exalted those of low degree; he has filled the hungry with good things, and the rich he has sent away empty."

Faith means discovering the content, basis and fulfillment of one's life in God, trusting entirely in him, and building on him alone. Faith means taking God's road and letting oneself be commissioned by him in service for others. Mary is a shining and inviting example of what such a life lived from faith can be.

We need that kind of orientation today and need it urgently when we are experiencing an appalling lack of purpose and a hitherto unimagined lack of direction. The days leading up to Christmas are exactly the right time for us to ask what the sources of our life are, and what direction, basis and meaning it should have. Otherwise, it could happen that at Christmas, when we have done everything possible to celebrate the feast in a fitting and pleasing framework, we suddenly feel a great inner emptiness and are quite let down. Mary is our sign of how life can be fulfilled from a basis of faith, and how faith can put things right: other than by means of outward show, outward security and outward riches. It is imperative that we should remember all this, but we would be foolish to see such external things as the fulfillment and purpose of life, or even merely as the meaning of Christmas.

2. Model of the community of the faithful

Mary had to make her decision on her own, and often enough had to make her own way in the face of various instances of incomprehension and misunderstanding. But she could not do that alone. In faith we have to rely on the community which supports us and which we ourselves support. You cannot be a Christian on your own.

It is in such a state that Mary goes on her way. She goes to visit her cousin Elizabeth with whom she shares the secret of her hope. Elizabeth, too, has been chosen by God in a special way. She too is to be a sign of the grace, mercy and life-giving power of God. Something very simple yet very profound must have happened when the two women met — something that the Bible expresses in a highly nuanced yet symbolic way. Something, so to speak, starts moving that releases joy and celebration. For the salvation promised by the Patriarchs, the Savior hoped-for in many difficult hours of history, is there. At this moment both women incorporate not only their faith but the hope of the entire people. They are both the beginning and the model of the new people of God.

Mary therefore is not only the model of the faith of the individual Christian but the model of the whole community of the faith, the primary model of the Church. Her faith makes her the gate whereby salvation enters the world and hence the mother of all the faithful. And so she enters into and remains together with mankind in God's history. She cannot be explained away from it or just excluded. All nations must call her blessed! Her image is the model for the election and vocation of all of us.

Therefore Mary is also a sign of faith in that we never have faith for ourselves alone but always enjoy it with others and for others. Faith gives us a place in the great history of hope which encompasses all humanity, and faith takes us into service for the sake of human hope. It includes us in the community of all the faithful, in the Church. And there such encounters as that which took place between Mary and Elizabeth must occur again and again: encounters in which our common hope is involved and in which, reciprocally, we offer ourselves to that common hope.

If we celebrate Christmas as the coming of salvation,

as the fulfilment of our hope, then Christmas may justifiably be thought of as an occasion of human and Christian community. It should be a stimulus to human and Christian encounter; an opportunity for us once again to have time for one another, when we can tell one another what ultimately supports us in our lives. We have to learn all over again how to talk about religious matters and to exchange our opinions and experiences in that regard. Particularly on feast days, we have to try within our families to be the Church on a small scale. Nevertheless Christmas should not be a mere withdrawal into a cosy, private and domestic sphere. It must also be an occasion of breaking out to the greater community of the Church (and indeed to the greater community of all mankind), and above all to responsibility for those who are without hope.

3. Model of joy on the basis of faith

Mary is also the model of faith in that she clearly shows us what the goal of our hope and the content of our joy are. She is not called blessed because she has done much and has gone a long way. She is known as blessed because she has faith. As a believer she knows that she is not the one who provides her own salvation and the salvation of others. Salvation as a form of human achievement would be a most insecure foundation and therefore a very weak form of hope. Ultimately men and women can only hope if they are unconditionally and absolutely accepted and confirmed, as unconditionally and absolutely as only God can pronounce them to be. This unconditional, unreserved Yes to mankind is something that God wished to assert in Jesus Christ; and it was this Yes of God that Mary received through her human Yes of faith. She knows that she is contained in this love of God, and that in it she finds the basis and content of her joy and her hope. Mary is the one who is wholly supported by God in faith, both in life and in death. Therefore she is able to say: "My soul magnifies the Lord, and my spirit rejoices in God my Savior."

Hence Mary is a sign that points not to herself but to God alone. An understanding of this should take the wind out of the sails of most objections to the honor we pay to Mary. Not a few people today have reservations and difficulties when they hear people talking about Mary and the honor paid to her. They are afraid that any emphasis on the figure of Mary could obscure the center of our Christian faith, which is the salvation of God in Christ Jesus. They think that to honor Mary is an unnecessary if not a rather unhealthy excrescence on the tree of Christian faith.

We have to take these objections seriously. They are justified in the face of certain erroneous manifestations and excessive forms of respect for Mary. But they do not affect the essential feature: Mary as the sign and image of a faith which is wholly centered on God. Hence Mary does not obscure Christ for us but directs us to him, and in fact brings him to us. She does not do that in so many words but by witnessing with her whole life to security and joy and on the basis of faith.

Joy is a topic that is especially close to us before Christmas. Often enough at this time of year we say to one another: "Merry Christmas!" Of course that is often said and meant rather superficially. But there is something very profound in this expressed wish: the desire for fulfillment of life, for joy and peace, which comes from communion with God. The Psalms state that this joy arising from faith is our strength. And it is this joy that we should wish one another in this Christmas season. Mary can act as a pointer for us on this way to joy. She is the model of our faith and of our hope.

II
The Humanity and Spirituality of Christian Joy
Advent: Philippians 4:4-9

THERE ARE NOT many things which we can still agree on in our pluralist society. One of the very few which people still have in common today (and which they have always had in common) is that all people want to be happy. Thomas Aquinas even goes so far as to say that we cannot *not* want happiness.

Yet what is happiness? We all know that we can have very different ideas of what it is. They range from the primitive satisfaction of physical impulses, through the securing of external needs of existence, to the good fortune of human love, artistic and spiritual or intellectual creation, and religious experience. Kant in his old age somewhat sourly remarked that the notion of happiness was a wholly undefined idea because everyone understood it in a different way. For Kant not striving for happiness but the fulfilment of duty was the highest of all things. But only a philosopher could think of an idea so distant from real human minds. To be happy is what we are all after.

1. The message of Christian joy

But what has this human happiness to do with Christianity and the Church? One of the most common objections to the claims of Christianity is that it is against all happiness and human joy. It is said that Christians throw suspicion on the guiltless joys and pleasures of the world and in that way poison them. Wherever people actually enjoy their lives Christianity interferes with its commandments: "Thou shalt not!" Christians, they say, have taken the joy out of life, At best, Christianity offers only that sublime heavenly kind of joy which "men of God" talk of so piously and sweetly, and which easily has a rather tedious and standoffish effect, like the euphoria of a harmless, balanced but essentially dead person. But that real kind of gut laughter which brings tears to the eyes, the kind of joy that makes one want to move mountains or jump over chairs, is something that most people think has little or nothing to do with Christian faith.

Did you enjoy the service? you are liable to be asked in America. In Europe the answer would be long faces treating it as an inappropriate question. Christianity is concerned with the high seriousness of life but not with the joys of life. Is that really the case? Has Christianity nothing to contribute to the ultimate, most profound thing which concerns all men and women? If that is so then what they say about Christians is true.

But the apostle Paul evidently thinks otherwise. The call to "rejoice" runs through the entire letter to the community in Philippi, and anyone who has even a superficial knowledge of the New Testament knows how often joy is mentioned in it. The angel brings the shepherds of Bethlehem the message of a great joy which applies to all mankind.

The Humanity and Spirituality of Christian Joy

The sermon on the mount begins with a series of blessings. The resurrected Christ says: "Peace be with you." Hence Paul's words are no more than an echo of this message of joy.

We cannot justifiably say that in those days they could laugh and rejoice without trouble or care; but that today, when there is so much injustice and suffering in the world, things are different. No, when Paul wrote his letter to Philippi, he was in prison; and a prison in those days was quite different from a modern jail — which is far from being a rest home. When Paul wrote his letter to the Philippians, he was suffering because he could not preach the gospel and because his communities were in danger. He must have expected his death sentence. Yet again and again he writes: "Rejoice, and yet again I say to you, rejoice!" And the reason for his joy was: "The Lord is near."

When I read those words I think once again of Easter 1970 when 2,500 young people from thirty-five different countries came to Taizé in France — a little village in Burgundy — the location of an ecumenical religious community. In his address Prior Roger Schutz said: "The risen Christ comes to make a feast live in the very heart of men and women." He announced a council of youth as the means and instrument of living this good news. It was to be opened that summer by more than thirty thousand young people.

Hence Christian joy is more than just theory. It is a lived and experienced reality. It was so then, and it is so now. It is the fundamental message of the gospel, the news of the joy that has come through Jesus Christ. But what, more exactly, is this Christian joy?

2. The humanity of Christian joy

Christian joy comprises all human joy and all human happiness. We should seize everything that is true, worthy and genuine, whatever is pure, deserving of love, noble, courageous, and praiseworthy. Christian joy is something profoundly human.

Only a man or woman can really rejoice. A dog can of course wag its tail. Then we are accustomed to say that the dog is happy or enjoying itself. But can a dog laugh? An anthropologist and philosopher called Helmut Plessner has shown in a famous book about laughing and crying that there is more to laughing and crying than a mood of the kind we can evoke with a little alcohol. Joy, he claims, is grounded in the "eccentric" position of mankind: in other words, in human freedom, in the human ability to distance oneself from oneself, from others and from the world; to release oneself, and by standing some way from the reality of the world to take it seriously. When one does that, suddenly many things no longer appear quite so serious and so important. Some things even seem rather comic and, taken the right way, even witty. So many very serious matters when seen in the right light are things one can only laugh at.

But this laughter is very ambiguous. There is a wild kind of laughter that goes with certain jokes. People who are conscious of their own dignity often find this laughter rather childish. But even such funny things are serious. This kind of laughter can have a curative effect. Of course there is another kind of laughter: cynical and ironic, or sarcastic, which makes and shows other people up as ridiculous. There is the laughter of the sceptic and the laughter of the desperate. And there is *Schadenfreude,* that ultimate

The Humanity and Spirituality of Christian Joy

pleasure which some people consider to be the most pure kind of joy. There are very primitive everyday pleasures which tend to make people rather vulgar. Goethe remarked that people can stand nothing less easily than a succession of good days. That kind of banal joy soon becomes boring and turns into a feeling that life is just tedious.

And there is another kind of joy: that felt at times of profound fulfilment when our heart expands and for a moment we feel content with ourselves and the world. In such moments laughter turns easily to tears; in other words, people lose their distance and poise. They are as it were overpowered and undone. It is not so much that one is the source of one's own joy as that happiness overcomes and grips one. Such moments of joy as seizure by a sudden coincidence of mankind and the world are seldom experienced. However, they reveal something very important: the greatest joy is only possible when people at least for a moment feel integrated into an overall context of meaning; when the tragic conflicts they suffer and usually cannot resolve suddenly dissolve; when for a moment something akin to joy breaks out in them. This kind of joy is profoundly connected with religion. Feast and festivity play a decisive role in the religions of all peoples, because in them something breaks out from the all-embracing context of meaning, something that we have to use the word God to describe.

If God is not the basis of joy and only human beings are to the fore, then everything becomes a human achievement, and joy is only recreation, a mere space in which to recover strength and breath for work. Leisure is no longer festivity but recreation. The world of work has taken complete control. In the Hitler period in Germany there was an organization with the revealing slogan, "Strength through Joy." But even if we do not take inhumanity as far as the Nazis, we can hardly say that festive occasions and days in our secularized society offer us any real joy. They usually fade out in their own festiveness. Most people do not really know how they ought to behave on such occasions. Our scientific and technological society is something we can plan and control; in principle it is without any surprises. It is an achieving society. It has no answer to the question of the meaning of the whole thing. At this point it abandons the individual. Feasts and festivity in our society have taught us how not to be joyful.

Only God liberates mankind from the duty of having to do everything, from the impulse to take ourselves too seriously and even play God and prophet. He liberates us from idolizing, absolutizing and ideologizing things. But that does not mean that religion makes people and the world of no value. It does not support the latterday gnosis which despises the world and finds it essentially decadent, only good enough to be smashed. Religion upholds a profound sympathy between all things and all men and women. It does not smooth over anything. It does however again and again make it possible to experience the little, insignificant things as the gift and creation of God. It can praise the cool water and the light of the sun with the words of St. Francis' hymn to the sun. With the psalms religion is able to praise God on account of wind and tempest, heat and cold. All those things for the believer are signs and symbols. What is joy if it is not praise of God because he alone allows mankind to be human!

I believe that we all must once again concern ourselves

more with true human culture, with the culture of joy — the joy that comes ultimately from faith. This humanity of joy does not exclude but includes everyday joys. But it does not find its ground in the outer regions of human existence, such as enjoyment, but in the profoundest center of the human being. It is to be found only in recollection from that central point; in spiritual attentiveness, and in concern for the ultimate, all-embracing meaning of our existence, in what is possibly an unspoken but perhaps thereafter intensive encounter with God.

3. The spirituality of Christian joy

The foregoing has allowed us preliminary access to the meaning of Paul's "Rejoice, for the Lord is near." We have greater need of such means of access today than in the past since we can longer simply presuppose the existence of religion and faith. Nowadays we have to make an even greater effort to understand Paul himself. It is a question here not only of the humanity of joy but of its spirituality.

This spirituality of joy, which Paul himself maintained even under threat of death, is founded upon the fact that God, whom we have aimed at as the ultimate horizon, was for Paul a very specific God: God as he had revealed himself in Jesus Christ and as he has come lastingly close to us "in the Lord." For Paul this God is himself joy. This God has given himself to be experienced as grace, which is loving kindness, splendor and glory, and as love which bestows itself freely. It is said of this God that he rejoices over the sinner who is converted and that he prepares joy in heaven for all men. This God rejoices over every one of us because he knows everyone by his or her name and loves everyone. It is said of this God that he laughs over the transgressor. He laughs, not because the suffering of the world leaves him unmoved, but because he is assured of his victory and of his rule.

For us God's laughter is a joyous message. It declares that the last word in human history does not belong to hatred, lies and injustice. It declares that in the end the murderer will not triumph over his victim but that in the end truth, justice, and God's peace and joy will be triumphant. A Christian's joy is merely the echo of this joy and laughter of God which offer to all history the judgment of God, the God who accepts, acknowledges and loves every man and woman who is ready to receive his acceptance, acknowledgment and love, and who rejoices over every one, even the loneliest of us.

I think that it should be clear by now that this Christian joy is far from an ineffectual and naively affirmative attitude. In fact, it is impossible to conceive of anything more critical than Christian joy. It derides all those presumed values and idols which are so prevalent in our times. This joy arises from an incomparable degree of nonconformity. It is quite different from the everyday ideals of human happiness. Blessed are those who mourn for they shall rejoice! If we take the statements of the Sermon on the Mount seriously we shall find that they comprise an alternative to the *status quo.* Nevertheless Christian joy also has a reconciliatory power. It enables us to accept others and ourselves because we ourselves and all others are accepted absolutely. In this light there is no situation that can be essentially hopeless. It is in this all-conquering power that Paul can say: "I have learned, in whatever state I am, to be content. I know how to be abased, and I know how to abound; in any and all circumstances I have learned the secret of facing plenty and

The Humanity and Spirituality of Christian Joy 25

hunger, abundance and want. I can do all things in him who strengthens me."

We find the same joy in other "great" believers. For St. Francis it suddenly became so powerful that he simply picked up two sticks and used them to play, dance and sing as if he held a fiddle and bow in his hands. Francis Xavier was so joyful that he behaved like a child and threw an apple into the air and caught it, at a time when it was bitterly cold in Japan, he was deprived of everything that makes life pleasant, and the victim of failure.

What makes someone behave like that? What makes a person talk like Paul? To be sure, joy is seldom so overpoweringly strong. It is usually a note of festivity, trust and confidence. But how is that possible? Not through some kind of performance or effort, or as the result of special religious techniques, forms of meditation or ascetic practices. Joy has to be a gift. Joy has to be God himself; God who gives himself to us, who offers himself to us for enjoyment and for joy. I do not mean that ironically, and of course not cynically. On the contrary. That is the language of Christian mysticism, the language of an experience of profound security, of being supported and enfolded, of a deep comfort and inner happiness that can encompass a person who is ready to open himself or herself to them.

Paul calls this joy a fruit of the Spirit. The Spirit is God's overflowing joy: the power that Paul sees at work in the whole creation; the strength that enables him to draw everything to him; the power that comes to the aid of our longing and hoping and brings them to undreamed-of fulfillment. The Spirit is God himself in his grace and love; in the excess and outpouring of his love which he will use to fulfill all things in order eventually to usher in the kingdom of freedom. This Spirit is bestowed on all the baptized. According to Paul it dwells in our hearts and fills us with a peace that surpasses all understanding. According to Paul, a Christian is someone who allows himself or herself to be impelled by this Spirit — or, we might say, by this joy. Nowadays we can see that same Spirit at work in a number of novel spiritual movements all over the world. We may hope that this Spirit will renew the Church, the world, and our own lives. And such a renewed life and such a renewed Church will be before all else a Church and a life of joy. But we have to open ourselves to this joy; we have to become spiritual men and women in the true sense of the word.

Roger Schutz's words are relevant here: "The risen Christ comes to make a feast live in the very heart of men and women. He makes ready for us a springtime of the Church which no longer possesses any means of power and is ready to share with all, and is a place of visible community for all mankind. He will give us enough imagination and courage to prepare a way to reconciliation. He will make ready our lives and affect them so that people no longer make men and women their victims."

It is not yet appropriate, and it is in fact quite impossible clearly to sketch what such a life lived out of joy in the Spirit might be. But in order to invoke this Spirit it is necessary to pray fervently and constantly. We are promised that the Spirit will answer prayer; indeed prayer is a fruit of the Spirit. And so prayer is the source of joy in the Holy Spirit. Paul says: "Have no anxiety about anything, but in everything by prayer and supplication with thanksgiving let your requests be made known to God. And the peace of God, which surpasses all understanding, will keep your hearts and your minds in Christ Jesus."

III
The Word is made Flesh
Christmas: John 1:14

1. Feast of everyday Christian life

A FAMILIAR EXPERIENCE for most people is that among all the rush and turmoil of the days before Christmas the one thing missing is the Christmas mood or feeling itself. The general busyness of the weeks leading up to Christmas instead of preparing us for Christmas and directing us toward it has a somewhat negative effect. Someone said to me once: "Christmas as a Christian feast is dead. We have killed it off. It's too late to do anything about it. If we are not careful, once the feast is past everything is the same as before. What does all the fine language really mean?"

When I re-read the Christmas story in the Gospel recently, it suddenly occurred to me that things really were not any different then. Christmas did not happen where the festivity and celebration were taking place, in the Temple at Jerusalem; and not where the major political decisions were being made, in Rome, the center of the Roman Empire. Even then Christmas "happened" in the midst of the world's everyday life, under very ordinary, quite unpretentious conditions. It occurred in the middle of the turmoil of an unsuccessful search for a lodging which had to be improvised in the cattle-shed at Bethlehem. There was certainly nothing sentimental about the first Christmas.

However, in the midst of wholly unfestive, sombre, everyday life something happened which can be expressed only imprecisely and with the aid of imagery; something quite incomprehensible and quite incredible. The Word became flesh. God himself entered into our everyday life in a wholly insignificant way. He became man and like to us in every respect except for sin. He assumed not only the magnitude and dignity of human existence but the ordinary, banal character of everyday human life.

Christmas is the feast of everyday Christian life. It is the most human of all feasts. It teaches us to look for and to find God not in the exceptional but in the unexceptional, not at sacred heights and in exalted moods but in the average and ordinary. Since God became man, there is no longer any human situation and no human area which is essentially godless or removed from God. Since then God lives not only in temples or in churches, but his glory has become apparent among us. Since God became man, humanity, everyday human life, has been the place where we meet God.

2. The human feast

But what is man? Man or humanity is *the* theme nowadays. Everyone seems to talk about humanizing cities, schools and workplaces. Everyone seems to be agreed that it is not a matter of general principles but of what affects the human individual. Quite right. But perhaps there has seldom been so much inhumanity as there is today. Torture is quite common in ninety states around the globe. In many countries freedom is suppressed, and people are imprisoned merely because they think and talk differently from those who are in charge or run the place. Two-thirds of mankind live below the minimum subsistence level and cannot lead a really human life. The reader of this book probably lives in a free and rich country. Yet we contribute to the poisoning of our environment, to such a degree that it becomes ever less human. In spite of external prosperity there is much unacknowledged internal and external need, loneliness, resignation and despair. What value do we place on humanity if we are beginning to manipulate human birth and death?

But what is man? The essential crisis of our times is probably that we no longer have a common answer to this question. In our age man himself has become problematic. Everyone senses that if he recollects himself for a moment and heeds his own life: Who am I actually if I remove the many masks behind which I hide? What am I here for? To what end do I work and strive? What is left in the end? What is the meaning of human existence?

If we ask such questions, we realize that man is a pointer into a profound mystery. This mystery is no puzzle or problem. It is possible to solve puzzles and problems over and over again. But man is a question to which he himself can give no answer. His mystery is so profound that it is possible to answer it only by invoking the notion of God. Man's heart is so large that only God is big enough to fill it. Therefore, there is no answer to the question of the humanization of our world and our life other than the renewal of faith in God. Only a new respect for God can substantiate a new respect for man. The purely human on the other hand moves in a closed circle and is hopelessly subject to death. Hence the nineteenth-century proclamation of the death of God led logically to the twentieth-century proclamation of the death of man.

The message of Christmas is that God lives and that he has accepted man. Christmas means that the fulness of God has entered into the empty openness of man. The God-man Jesus Christ is the ultimate answer to the quest and question of man, and to the questions posed by men nowadays. Therefore, it is idiotic to maintain that it is possible to make belief in Jesus Christ more appropriate to modern man by effacing or playing down his true divine nature and presenting Jesus as no more than a sympathetic man committed to God and to his fellow men. If Jesus Christ were only a man and nothing but a man then he could offer us only that which is human — human in all its finiteness and restriction. Then we would not be redeemed in our deepest need, the need of sin and death. But because Jesus is God, by him hope has entered our history, by him a road leads into openness and freedom, and the future is disclosed to us.

Through Jesus Christ we know finally that our human life does not vanish into a desert of nothingness, but retains lasting value and dignity. Through Jesus we know that we are accepted absolutely and ultimately as only God can affirm and love. Therefore, Christmas is the feast of mankind; the feast that finally discloses and presents us with true human scope and true human dignity.

3. The feast of Christian brotherhood

No human being exists for himself or herself alone. Every

The Word is made Flesh

one of us is a human being together with other human beings. At home in the family, at work, in public, and wherever we happen to be. All mankind comprises a great community with its own destiny. Today we know more precisely than in the past that as human beings we are all in the same boat. There is a great solidarity of guilt and of hope. God entered into this solidarity through Jesus Christ. Since then, every human existence has been defined by the fact that Jesus Christ is a member of the same species as every man and woman, and every man's and woman's fellow citizen, fellow human being, and brother. God's becoming man has therefore changed something in the life of all men. The beginning of a new humanity has been located in the midst of history, a beginning in which man is no longer man's enemy but man's brother. The seed of a new, fraternal humanity has been laid down in Jesus Christ. In him hope came into the world, not only for the individual but for the human community as a whole and for human life together in the spirit of humanity. Christmas is the feast of human brotherhood.

This understanding is especially important in our present situation. Roger Schutz, the Prior of Taizé, put this notion of Christian brotherhood at the mid-point of his second letter to the people of God. He wrote this letter from Calcutta; from one of the great conurbations of the world where the problems of mankind today are especially urgent. The contrast between rich and poor nations is a major challenge to Christian brotherhood at the present time. In the last few centuries we in the West have developed a way of thinking and living which stresses the individual and his personal freedom. That has brought to light numerous values from which we cannot and do not wish to retreat. What we have to realize today is that freedom is not only a personal good, and that the goods of the earth exist essentially for all men. No part of what we have is for us alone. Everything that we have has been given to us by God, by the God who deprived himself of all riches in order to enter into the poverty of a human being. Surely it is the duty of us Christians to act likewise.

At Christmas every year we notice how life changes, if only for a few hours we behave in a human and friendly way to each other, if we give ourselves to one another, and if we are merely human to one another. The question is whether this is only a short idyll and a pious illusion or whether Christmas should not be something more than that: in other words, whether it should not be a model and a spur to brotherliness as a universal standard of behavior. The question whether we are prepared to see and to encounter Jesus Christ himself in the poorest of the world also decides whether we are serious about behaving as Christians in the everyday world.

Nowadays we are in need of a double conversion: conversion to God without whom man is lost, and conversion to our neighbor, without whom we cannot find God. Both go together. Love of God and love of our fellow man, or as Schutz puts it: struggle and contemplation. Both are part of being a Christian: struggle for a more just and more human world; a struggle which draws its strength from encounter and community with God. Since God became man, we can meet God only in man; but we can encounter man in his real profundity only when we meet God in him. Jesus Christ the God-man reveals both to us: the mystery of God and the mystery of man. He summons us to a fraternal form of being a Christian in the everyday world.

God himself took the first step and gave us the beginning

of a new humanity and a new mankind. He put down a new basis and thereby gave us ground for hope. Therefore, we should celebrate Christmas festively; we should sing and be happy. A light has shone in the midst of this world's darkness. The world's night has become a holy night. It is illumined by the light of God's love. Therefore, it is no longer a sinister, threatening night but a night in whose peacefulness the sacred has opened up a space for itself. It has become a holy and a peaceful night in which God's glory is reflected in a human face.

IV
Repentance as the Way to Christian Freedom

Lenten Penance: Mark 1:14-15

LENT HAS COME round again. Many readers will immediately ask what meaning penitence can have today. We should not seek to obscure the fact that the Christian understanding of penitence and Christian practice in that regard are in a profound state of crisis. When at this time I hear again and again the call to repentance in the texts of the Mass, I have a guilty conscience, or at least I feel somewhat dishonorable. In fact there is more or less no generally practiced order of fasting, and confession has diminished considerably in the last decade. I am not mentioning this in order to complain. Certainly the old form of penitence and confession was not only of service to Christian freedom. It also produced anxiety and unfreedom. A deep-reaching reform was required. We cannot and do not want to bring back the old ways. But in present conditions we cannot just remain where we are and look on this with satisfaction. Right now, at the start of Lent, we have to make a new beginning. I should like to consider this new start in the following terms: penitence as the way to Christian freedom.

1. The dignity of the person

A new beginning is prompted first by a purely anthropological consideration — one directed, therefore, to mankind. Today the problem is not only confession and repentance. Something much more basis is in danger of being lost: an awareness of responsibility and hence a consciousness of what constitutes the dignity of the human person.

The Würzburg synod in Germany describes our situation when it says that profession of the Christian faith today "concerns a society which is constantly engaged in trying to liberate itself from the notion of guilt. With its talk of sin and guilt Christianity resists that implicit wave of guiltlessness which is spreading through our society and which causes us, if at all, always to look for guilt and error in "others," in our enemies and opponents, in the past, in nature, in heredity and environment. The history of our freedom seems bifurcated. An uncanny guilt mechanism takes effect in it. We ascribe the successes to ourselves, but otherwise we cultivate the art of repression, the denial of our responsibility, and we constantly go in search of new alibis in regard to the dark, catastrophic and unhappy aspects of the history which we ourselves make and write.

"This implicit wave of guiltlessness also concerns our interpersonal relations. It does not demand but rather increasingly endangers responsible commerce with others. It subjects interpersonal conditions to the questionable ideal of a freedom which presumes on the guiltlessness of a natural egotism. But this kind of freedom does not liberate; instead it strengthens the loneliness and anomie of people living in the same society."

Here we are concerned with nothing less than the loss of the very dimension of humanity: of the human person and his or her responsibility. We are concerned with the destruction of that which is human, and to some extent with an explicit and openly asserted antihumanism. In this situation the Church has to act as the advocate of mankind. In doing so the Church has to remind people that human dignity consists in being aware of oneself, in possession of self, and dedicated to the proper expression of self. Man is responsible for his actions. He forgoes his human dignity if he does not fulfil his responsibility but discards it. The call to repentance is intended to remind us of this responsibility, to make us conscious once again of our dignity as human beings. No one should declare that penitence is something suitable only for backwoodsmen and lovers of the obsolescent and obsolete. Repentance is what is required today; it is a wholly modern thing.

2. Repentance and the center of the Christian message

Our anthropological reflection, our thoughts on the human implications of the matter, should be followed by theological reflection, and by that I mean thought orientated to the Gospel. Here we should be guided by the Gospel for the day. It is one of the most important and fundamental texts of the entire New Testament. In it Mark summarizes the whole of Jesus' program. It is important to note that these "basic guidelines" talk of conversion and repentance.

For Jesus, of course, conversion and repentance are not subsidiary matters but quite central. They are unconditional aspects of being a Christian. But that also means that conversion and repentance have to do with the Gospel, with the good news, according to which God's rule and kingdom are imminent. Hence conversion and repentance are not some kind of achievement, a task and a burden, something unpleasant, sad and distasteful. They are an essential part of the good, the happy news of the coming of God's rule and kingdom.

What does that mean? It means that the hope of mankind is beginning to be realized; that our hope of justice, truth, peace, and freedom is being fulfilled. Ever since there have been people on earth, there have been injustice, lies and the use of force. But mankind has never ceased to hope that in the end the killers, liars and powermongers will not have the last word. Yet whenever they began to produce order from their own resources, they had to use some kind of force. In so doing they sowed the seeds of new hatred and new injustice which from the start poisoned the new order they sought to impose. Hence people moved in a continuous vicious circle of force and counterforce, of guilt and revenge. How was it possible to emerge from this fateful situation other than by a new beginning, one that might come not from man's guilt-ridden history, but from above and only from "above": from God. Only God could introduce the hoped-for kingdom of truth and justice, of peace and freedom. Therefore, Jesus announces in the Fourth Gospel the fulfilment of mankind's hope, the fulness of time. He says that man's seeking and struggle, his labor and concern, are not in the end meaningless. God has taken to himself the hoping and expectation of his suffering creature.

Repentance is nothing other than entrusting oneself to this very new beginning. But it is impossible to turn to the new without turning aside from the old. Therefore, repentance means making oneself free of the power of the old; liberating oneself from the existing standards and plausibility, from what one says, does, thinks, and expects, in order to become free for truth, justice, peace, and freedom which come to us from God. To repent therefore means conversion; it means a new turn on the steering wheel of one's life, a new direction away from the old and toward the new, for the sake of the future of that new life which God bestows upon us and which is God himself.

Surely that is a message for us today, for we often despair in the future and resign ourselves to the experience of an inner emptiness and an insufferable absence of meaning. Much that is frequently criticized as pleasure-seeking is essentially no more than despair in the future, a lack of courage in the face of greater goals. Lent is intended to shake us up, to give us courage, and to remind us of our dignity as human beings and of the center of our Christian life: the coming of the rule and kingdom of God which make us free to lead true Christian lives; a form of human existence which does not mean enslavement to the things of the world, but rejoicing in the freedom of things and of the world, and which uses that freedom in the service of our own vocation.

3. The practice of repentance

Finally I offer a more practical reflection, yet without giving any precise recipe for practice. If freedom is in question there can be no hard-and-fast guidelines. One can do no more than suggest the direction and the possibilities of a realization of Christian freedom. Therefore, I keep to the traditional formula of faith, hope and charity.

1. Repentance as an expression of Christian faith. Faith is more than a profession of articles of faith. And more does not mean less! Hence faith in the full sense means trusting wholly in the reality of God, surrendering oneself to it, building on it and basing life on it. Sin on the other hand is an attempt to ensure one's life falsely and to fulfill it erroneously: by money, power, knowledge, achievement, sensual pleasure, and so on. Sin by such means denies that God alone is the ultimate ground and ultimate goal of mankind. Repentance means discarding such false things, those attitudes which negate the meaning of existence. Repentance means taking conversion to God as the ultimate and ultimately decisive reality of our lives. In repentance, therefore, we are asked on what we build our lives, where we are going or think we are going, and where we look for happiness and fulfilment. We are asked when we do penance whether we really believe and whether we treat our belief seriously.

2. Penitence as an expression of Christian hope. No one can live without hope; no one can work or love without hope. This hope was given to us anew through Jesus Christ and his message of the coming of God's rule and kingdom. Through Jesus Christ man knows that he is ultimately supported in living and in dying. This hope can be traduced in two ways: by anticipating fulfillment, when a person thinks he can fulfill his life by himself, when he thinks all things are possible, are manipulable. Christian piety has always called that attitude pride. But it is also possible to traduce Christian hope by anticipating non-fulfillment: by the lack of courage which no longer dares

to do anything, but resignedly, despairingly and dully remains with the old ways and satisfied with everyday behavior. This little courage, this despondency, resignation and depression are just as dangerous nowadays as the pride that says life without God is quite possible. Hope resists lack of courage as it does pride. Hope is the great courage which looks to the ultimate, and for that reason discards the penultimate. But not so that the things of this world are despised and everything is left to trust in the hereafter. Because hope possesses a broader and greater perspective, it affords that inner distance which alone makes us free, so that things do not hold and use us but we possess and apply things in freedom. The real courage of hope gives us a great and generous heart which does not diminish through personal egotism but has room for the major things in life.

3. *Repentance as an expression of love.* Love is the fundamental idea of God's rule and kingdom and the sum of the whole gospel. It is the inner fulfillment of Christian freedom. Being free does not mean doing whatever one wants. Anyone who acts thus is essentially unfree; he merely enslaves himself to the passing moment and to his idle fancy. He or she is free who is also free from self, who can advance beyond the confines of self and exist entirely for another. True freedom is to be found only in selfless love. Love is the antithesis of egotism which would realize and fulfill self at another's cost. Therefore, repentance is nothing other than the banishment of narrow and calcifying egotism by the practice of freedom in love, by the practice of giving and bestowing. Hence repentance is something positive. Love has many individual areas and dimensions in which it can be realized. Earlier a distinction used to be made between the charitable and spiritual

works of mercy. Charitable works of mercy are so to speak the offer of a helping hand: every gift or application of self for another or for our human society. Spiritual works are, say, a really encouraging word, a friendly greeting, time for a talk, for selfless, fraternal advice.

Hence there are several forms of repentance: time for prayer as an expression of faith, practice of distance from customary things by choice and prudence, and the practice of love in its many forms. Penitential services and the sacrament of penance (which we are invited to frequent especially in Lent) are the sum and high point of this everyday Christian penitence. They ought to remind us that we need penance not only as individuals, but as the community of the faithful. In the Lenten weeks all are asked to celebrate their penitence as the way and gift of Christian freedom.

In conclusion, let me remind you of the thrust of the Gospel: When John the Baptist had been imprisoned, Jesus went to Galilee and preached the gospel of the Lord: the time is fulfilled and the kingdom of God is near at hand. Repent and have faith in the good news!

V
"Do this in memory of me"
Maundy Thursday: I Corinthians 11:23-26

WHENEVER WE CELEBRATE the eucharist, we hear the text for today's reading: "In the night in which he was delivered up . . ." On Maundy Thursday itself this text has an especially emphatic message for us. At this time we experience that memorable night in which all this happened, in a most extraordinary way. Therefore, we must very carefully consider the most important statements in this text, which is among the oldest in the New Testament.

"In the night in which he was delivered up!" It is the night of treachery by a friend and disciple, who delivers Jesus up to his enemies as he kisses his hands. It is the night in which the entire depths of evil were revealed in a flat *no* to God's truth and love and in a *no* to a friend to whom loyalty was owed. This evil exists in our world and in us. It is a profound mystery how men can be so evil and deny God and one another.

Yet this is not the real mystery of this night. Jesus is not quite passively delivered up to the powers of lies and force. He delivers himself up, and surrenders himself quite actively. "This is my body, which is given for you!" He freely gives his body, in other words, his life, his whole person, for us, He is not vanquished by the power of evil; he overcomes evil by means of love which bestows and gives itself. Hence evil is conquered by Jesus' own voluntary self-surrender.

Once sin has destroyed the covenant between man and God and between men, a new covenant is drawn up in Jesus' blood. By a new covenant we mean that in spite of our sin we are accepted, affirmed, loved, and reconciled. Our sins are forgiven us. A hand is stretched out which holds and supports us and joins us all one to the other all over again. The mystery of this night is the mystery of the greater love which overcomes evil and allows a new beginning.

In this way everything has become new for all time. Therefore, Jesus establishes a memorial of his saving action. "Do this in memory of me." The breaking of the bread is intended henceforth to be a sign of his broken body and of his self-sacrificing love; the sharing out of the bread and wine is to be a sign of his love by which he gives and communicates himself. As often as we do this, we announce the death of the Lord until he comes again. For as we look back we also look into the future, and anticipate in the sacramental sign the ultimate reconciliation of God and the world. Every celebration of the Eucharist is an actualization of redemption and a pre-celebration of its fulfillment in the kingdom of God. By means of the figures of bread and wine, Jesus is present among us, in order to allow his unique covenant to take effect in us, in order to reconcile us with God and with one another. Hence the eucharist joins and summarizes everything: the salvation established then, the future fulfillment of salvation, and the salvation which we share in today and in this place. Hence the eucharist is the high point and source of the life of a Christian and of the Church.

We should be thankful that in our century we have rediscovered the full richness of this mystery. This happened with the liturgical movement of the first half of the century, and was then confirmed by the second Vatican Council and extended to the whole Church. This did not mean the creation of a new mass but a rediscovery of the original and old mass and its revitalization in a renewed form. When nowadays we experience the eucharist more as a meal, and when more than in the past we now invite everyone to treat this meal not only with pious respect but as participants, then we have once again taken seriously Jesus' foundational words that we should do this in his memory.

Yet the external form of the rite is insufficient. We have to become conscious of the entire profoundity of the mystery which is made present to us in this sign. Paul says that we should distinguish this bread from any other bread and examine ourselves before we approach the Lord's table. For the principal thing is that the transformation of the bread and the wine should continue in the transformation of our lives; that the distribution of the bread should not be restricted to the church; that those who enter it to eat should be wholly seized by Jesus Christ; that they should receive Jesus Christ wholly and allow themselves to be seized by him in all his reality. In the washing of feet Jesus Christ gives us a practical example of what is meant here. He, the Lord, does the work of a slave. He reverses the arrangements of the world and gives us an example of how we should behave. We too should vanquish evil by good in the power of Christ's holy action.

It is possible to reflect for a long time on the words of today's text; in fact, there could be no end to such reflection. The right reaction is not really thought but thanksgiving. The text mentions that too. Jesus gave thanks when he took the bread and wine. He knew that all good gifts come from God. Thanksgiving is the proper expression of loving surrender. Therefore, we call the memorial celebration of Jesus' self-surrender to God, and for us, the celebration of the Eucharist — which means the celebration of thanksgiving. Thanks is due to God not least for the fact that he has given us this memorial of his love in Jesus Christ. And so let us give thanks to the Lord, our God. It is meet and right so to do.

VI
"He saw and believed"
Easter Sunday: John 20:1-9

1. The way to Easter faith

IF WE LISTEN attentively to the Easter Gospel, we can still sense something of the disarray of the first Easter morning. Mary Magdalen goes very early to the grave to mourn someone dear to her and to pay her last respects. To her astonishment the grave is empty. She imagines that someone must have opened it by force and removed the body. Distressed, she hurries off to the disciples. Peter and John want to see for themselves and find everything just as Mary described it. If we look into the other gospel accounts of these events we find various details reported differently. But one thing is constant in all accounts: the first witnesses of the resurrection were not easily convinced dreamers and visionaries. They did not fantasy and spin an Easter yarn, as it were. They checked everything critically. They must have passed through all the rigors of questioning and doubt, scepticism and resignation.

We all recognize ourselves in those disciples. On this Easter morning too the question is never quite silenced: Did it really happen? Will it be like that for us too one day? Should we really hope in a life after death? Perhaps the hard facts have the last word in the end. . . . The first disciples' doubts are our doubts too, and clearly we too as Christians are entitled to pose such questions honorably. All the more reason then for us to ask: How can we have sure and certain faith? On what is our Easter faith founded? How is it guaranteed?

The Gospel's answer is clear enough: "He saw and believed!" That is a remarkable answer. Does seeing lead to belief? For us, as modern men and women, the opposite seems to be the case. Many people think that more exact knowledge of facts and a more precise acquaintance with the causes of things in the real world must make faith more difficult, perhaps even superfluous, if not altogether impossible. What we see is that the dead no longer rise up, that in our time millions of human beings are refugees in Vietnam and Cambodia, and that hundreds of thousands of people are starving in Bangladesh and in the Sahel in Africa. Surely it is understandable that many should draw the conclusion that God is dead! After all, he was unable to save even the most just of all men, Jesus of Nazareth. How then is it possible for someone who sees things as they really are to have faith?

What kind of sight is it that leads to faith? It is the sight of the beloved disciple. We also know from our own experience that only superficial love makes us blind. True love makes us see. Whoever loves another sees more and sees more deeply. Only he or she who loves sees what is unique, what is worthy of love, in another human being. Whoever loves another will not write him or her off, even if everyone else deserts the loved one. Ultimately death does not subsume him or her. In the Old Testament the Song of Solomon says: "Love is stronger than death."

Love simply will not allow everything to be pointless and meaningless. Love hopes, and hopes for fulfillment of its love. Only he who is ready to pierce through the superficial dimensions and yardsticks of his life and to open himself up to what is greater than himself can touch, taste and hear; only that one who is ready to abandon egotism and to let go; only — in other words — whoever is prepared to think anew and to turn again can learn more and something more profound in the reality that lies before our eyes. For love knows that the reality that we can touch, taste and hear, quite externally, is not the sole, final and unique reality.

2. The content of Easter faith

Because of the empty grave the unique and ultimate reality suddenly hit John. Suddenly the scales, as it were, fell from his eyes. Suddenly he understood the words of Scripture that had been closed to him hitherto. Exegetes, or specialists in biblical science, argue about what passage in the Old Testament is referred to. But it is certainly not a question of this or that passage in the Bible, but of the fundamental message of Scripture. It testifies that God is not somewhere distant above the clouds where he rules undisturbed over a world full of terror and horror, but that God is rather a God of mankind who is present among us, in order to be here especially for the rejected, persecuted, poor, and suffering. According to the Old Testament, God is a God of life. He holds in his hands our transient life that nevertheless strives after the ultimate. He is Lord over life and death; yet he does not wish the death of any man or woman but only that he or she should live. Therefore, we must hope, even and indeed precisely in the midst of failure and death, to be sharers in the fullness of his life.

This basic experience of the Old Testament was fulfilled in Jesus of Nazareth in an unrepeatable way. Like no other he proclaimed God's rule of love and lived wholly out of trust in God his Father. God did not abandon him but strengthened his preaching and his life by receiving Jesus into the fullness of his own life. In this way he established a new beginning which allows us, too, to hope that in the end, life will prevail over death and love over hatred; that in the end not lies and force but God's truth and love will have the last word.

Hence belief in the resurrection is not something additional to our ordinary faith. It is the summary of our whole faith. Everything stands or falls with Easter. For whoever believes that God is, and that he is the ultimate, deepest all-inclusive reality that rules over all things, the mystery in which our existence loses itself; such a one may also be convinced that all that is fragmentary, dark and puzzling in our life is so to speak only the negative, the other side of a fullness of light and life. For it is merely the final consequence of this faith to assert that it encompasses even the power of death, so that we can join Paul in saying: "Whether we live or die we belong to the Lord." What happened to Jesus of Nazareth at Easter is not a unique miracle, but the beginning and ground of a new reality — the ultimate one.

Belief in the resurrection of Jesus therefore gives us a new insight into life's reality. It allows us to see in a new way: it gives us the light of faith. That does not mean that faith argues away any part of the harshness of everyday life, or the pain of suffering and death, or the brutality of history. Nothing is covered up! But everything that otherwise splits into meaningless fragments now comes together into a whole. Easter gives the dark side of our life a meaning. As Christians we are entitled to ask: Who can give us a better way of seeing than this Easter light? Whither should we go if not in this direction? Where else are we to find such words of life? Where else is there such a message with which we can live and die? Therefore, Easter is truly a day of thanksgiving and a day of joy.

3. The community of the faithful

The foregoing does not exhaust the Gospel. There is something more, perhaps rather covert, in today's Gospel. We have to read and listen attentively if we are to discover it. We have already learnt how the beloved disciple came first to the grave; his love led him first to the point of belief. Oddly enough, Peter, the representative of the Church and its office, came a little behind. But — and this is the decisive point — John drew back and let Peter take precedence. That, like so much in John's Gospel, is intended symbolically. It has to be stressed that it is not the isolated individual who finds faith by himself alone. In faith everyone is asked to remember that everyone else supports him in belief. Everyone is referred to the whole community of the faithful, to the Church which is represented by Peter. The sight that faith gives us is a communal experience.

Nowadays we find it difficult to draw back like John and to include ourselves without reservation in the church community. Criticism of the Church and its office-bearers is far from muted within the Church too these days. In fact the Church is a Church of sinners; otherwise, we should not belong to it. As a Church of sinners, it is worthy of criticism. But it is also the Church which has delivered the Easter light to us throughout the centuries. Only through the witness of the first Church, which was passed on through the centuries, do we know anything at all about Easter. The Church passes the faith onto us not by words but through the lives of untold numbers of Christians who devote everything, even their lives, to the new Easter life. The Church is not only the Church of sinners but the Church of saints, and also of the many unknown and unacknowledged saints of everyday life.

Easter is, I have said, a stimulus to praise and devotion. Easter is also a call to decisively join the ranks of the Church. We are all this Church. We are all charged with the mission of ensuring that in our world something becomes visible of the joy, life and hope of Easter. It is up to us to ensure that when people look at the Church they do not see an empty grave or perceive monuments of a faith that existed once upon a time, but see signs of new life. We should be the means by which they meet people who are looking not for what is below but what is above. We should be the means by which they see and believe.

We are gathered together here as the community of the faithful. As with the first disciples, the Lord wishes to be among us here by means of his words and the eucharistic meal. We too should be able to say: We have seen and therefore we believe. What we see is, as then, only faint signs. But those signs contain the power of the new life. In the midst of the transience of our life we are already granted the ultimate life. Therefore, this Eucharist should become the occasion of festivity and celebration. We should sing: Christ is risen, and so we must all rejoice.

VII
On the Road to Emmaus
Easter Monday: Luke 24:13-35

1. A way of questions

IT IS STRANGE. I can always hear the story of the disciples on their way to Emmaus and experience it anew. I never find it boring. It always has something new to say to me. Why is that?

The first thing I like in this story is the two disciples who put their questions so honestly: Why? Why has everything happened differently from what we expected? What happens now? What happened then? They receive no answer to these questions. No one can resolve their doubts, Yet the two disciples are full of courage. Their hope has proved sound. Now they return bravely to their everyday lives, to their families and to their work. They do not give up. They go on. Yet they are critical. They do not surrender to idle dreams and do not accept the women's story of an empty grave. They want to see and judge for themselves. The fact that both these men occur in the Gospel seems to me unusually comforting. For it shows that questions and doubts were not only possible but permitted in Jesus' circle. Faith is never simply a finished possession, a triumphalist certainty. It is questioning and disputed faith, faith that is on its way — on its way to Emmaus.

Hence the two disciples are an image of ourselves. For surely we too are often on the same road to Emmaus. On our life's road too there are questions and doubts to which there is no harmoniously closed answer. There are questions whose difficulties no one can easily solve. In our life too there is courageous persistence in everyday life. And all this has its place in faith. All this is part of being a disciple of Jesus Christ.

2. Jesus Christ — the unrecognized companion

But this story has a second part. This is the part that really fascinates me. Jesus is also on the same road. Hidden and unrecognized, yes, but he is certainly taking the same way. The disciples are as if struck blind. Their eyes are as if sealed but their hearts are fired when he interprets the Scripture for them. Power, profound warmth and a deep glow shine forth from him.

Here we are presented with the very reality of Easter. Before Easter the disciples awaited the coming of God's kingdom in splendor and glory; they hoped for the appearance of God's glory in all openness. They were astonished and shocked that it did not happen thus. But now their experience is that this hope was not fundamentally deceptive. It is merely that it has been fulfilled in another way: in the shape of the cross. In the resurrection of Jesus and in his entry into the glory of the kingdom of God the kingdom of God itself has arrived. It is now a living among us in the new presence of Jesus Christ through his Holy

Spirit. Therefore, the new is there under the husk of the old. God's riches under the form of human poverty; his fullness in the unmeaning emptiness of our questioning and doubt. Jesus Christ has not departed from us through his resurrection. He has come among us from God in a new way.

Surely the experience of the two disciples on the road to Emmaus is our experience too. In our lives too there are those who accompany us and through whom Christ is with us. Such people can be husband or wife, a friend, an acquaintance. But the Emmaus experience can also take the form of a fleeting encounter, a sudden word that gives us the power and courage to continue on our way and persevere. We are accompanied above all by the community of disciples, the Church, in which Jesus Christ is present through his Spirit in a special way. Hence there are many forms by which, unknown and often unacknowledged, Jesus Christ is present in our lives. But there are also many ways in which we can make Jesus Christ present for others by becoming their companions on the road and in life. Each of us can recall such episodes and such persons from his own experience, about whom he can say as a Christian that in this instance he experienced the closeness of Jesus Christ, of whom he can say that they kept the spark of life in his heart warm and alive, so that in the end the fire was not put out.

3. Word and sacrament as companions on the way

There is a third thing which makes this story of the two disciples so exemplary. The hidden presence of Jesus Christ could of course be suspected of being mere appearance, a pure illusion, if it were not constantly tangible and open to experience. It would remain empty and abstract if it were not constantly clear to us, at least in a symbolic form.

This symbolic revelation of Jesus Christ occurs in a dual guise: Jesus interprets the Scripture to the disciples and he breaks bread for them. The word and the sacrament are the two forms in which Christ becomes tangibly present to us in symbolic form. In the word of Scripture and in proclamation he becomes present in order to show us the meaning of our lives and in order to give us light, direction and perspective. In the eucharistic meal he gives us himself as the power of life, as the power by which we in return can give ourselves as free gifts. In the breaking of bread, in the celebration of the eucharist, we can know him most intensely, just as the disciples recognized him most clearly in that way.

Perhaps some people will now remark: the word is a more Protestant approach whereas the meal and eucharist sound more Catholic. In fact there was a time when the difference might be summarized thus. But, thank God, we have come a long way since then. Both divisions of the Christian Church recognize today more firmly than yesterday that the word and the sacrament belong together intimately and inalienably. Hence in the last twenty to thirty years the Catholic Church has discovered more profoundly the implications of the word of God, the meaning of Holy Scripture, the meaning of preaching, and Protestants are constantly placing the eucharist more and more at the center of divine service. This kind of emphasis on the eucharist or Lord's Supper is quite Biblical. Not only at this point but in many other places in the New Testament it becomes clear that the risen Christ appeared to his disciples during the meal and was present in that way. By his word and his sacrament he now wishes to give us the power, light and splendor of the new life in the midst of our own lives.

It is no accident that from the moment when Jesus became present to the two disciples in the meal, the mood changed utterly. Before it had been sad and depressed, but suddenly it became joyful. Joy and movement now enter the text. The disciples do not wish to keep the news to themselves but hurry back to Jerusalem. They have to tell the others and experience their acknowledgment that the Lord is really risen and has shown himself to Simon. Ultimately, then, the road to Emmaus is a way to joy. More than that, it is a road to common joy and celebration.

We must now celebrate and take together this way through questions and doubts, this way on which Christ is with us in a hidden form, the way on which he accompanies us through his word and his sacrament, and the way that leads to joy.

VIII
Experience of the Spirit
Pentecost: Romans 8:19-30

WHEN THE APOSTLE PAUL arrived at Ephesus during his third missionary journey and met some disciples there, he asked them: "Have you received the Holy Spirit?" They answered, somewhat disconcerted: "We have never heard of this Holy Spirit." Modern Christians would probably say, for the most part, "We have certainly heard of the Holy Spirit, but we have seen nothing of him." There are other spirits at work in our world whose traces we can see every day. What counts is not spirit, and not even the Holy Spirit, but facts, figures, money, power, achievement, prestige: the fulfillment of concrete human needs. We are all more or less affected by this spirit of practical materialism. When on the other hand experience of the Holy Spirit is in question, we have to acknowledge that the evidence is missing.

This is an alarming situation for us as Christians. For Paul, to possess the Holy Spirit and to be a Christian are identical. Paul defines Christians as those who are impelled by the Spirit. What sort of Christian life do we lead, then, if it features so little spiritual impulsion and event, and if we just go on living an unconcerned life without any tension, as tediously as any other people? What sort of Christians are we if we have nothing or almost nothing to recount of when and how in our lives we have experienced the vital power of the Spirit? No wonder if other people turn away from us in boredom!

1. The Spirit in the world

Paul names three areas in which he has experienced the Spirit of God and in which we too, if we lay ourselves open thus, can learn something of the action of the Spirit. First Paul looks into the world. It is full of unrest; it is in constant ferment, continually producing novelty. Everywhere there is expectation, hope and longing: longing for something more, hope in something better. But against all hope the world is also full of indifference and nullity; it is given up to decadence and corruption. It is subject to transience. Hence it moves to and fro between hope and fear. One might think that the apostle was describing our own situation nowadays. We live in a world which claims that it is dynamic, a world of constant development. In all areas of life there are extraordinary changes and new directions. But at the same time this world has no real goal. If we ask about the meaning of the whole vast undertaking we enter a vacuum. More and more, faster and faster. But why, wherefore, to what end? Surely everything is frighteningly unspiritual and therefore meaningless? Surely all of us behind our masks of optimism experience an existential anxiety that reaches right down into the depths of our being?

Yet Paul does not write off the world. He perceives something deeper in this unrest and in this futile hope. He calls it the groaning of the Spirit: the Spirit in travail.

Experience of the Spirit 61

He is convinced that in all the difficulties, dead ends, deceptions, and frustrations we may see the birth pangs of a coming realm of freedom. Hence in our world as it moves to and fro between hope and fear, Paul perceives the living action of the Spirit of God. That is the Creator Spirit — *Spiritus creator,* as the Pentecost hymn puts it. From the very beginning he has been at work in all reality in order to lead it toward the goal that God has ordained for it: the kingdom of freedom of the sons of God in the kingdom of God.

That is a really bold statement. We have to read it twice before we can believe that that is what is meant. But surely in all the unrest and in all the unsatisfactory circumstances of the world there is an excess of hope, an additional value which points to a greater and more profound mystery in our reality; one which shows that the real world that we touch, see, measure, plan, and form is not the sole and ultimate reality. A Christian is convinced that this intangible mystery which runs through all things, attracts us with its sense of hope and yet fills us with a certain anxiety is not an empty, meaningless wilderness of nothingness but creative life and divine Spirit; that which is to be found wherever among all the questions and problems, inadequacies and conflicts, something new and something better is sought for and fought for, wherever it is a question of more freedom and more justice, of peace and reconciliation; for there God's Spirit is at work.

That does not mean that the Holy Spirit is identical with the present fashion or that he is on the side of utopian enthusiasm. We define fashion as that which tomorrow is already out of date. Therefore, whoever weds the spirit of the age will soon be a widower or widow. Paul is talking about something else. He is telling us that we Christians should not retire into a ghetto; instead we should seek out among all the fashions of the time and their attendant idiocies the deeper concern which often lies hidden there. We should recognize the "signs of the times" and understand our situation as God's summons to us. We should test everything and keep what is good. For whatever in the world is always good, true and beautiful is of the Spirit of God. Therefore, as we co-operate in seeking, working and suffering together in this world of ours, we can experience something of the mystery of the Spirit of God.

2. The Spirit in the Church

Hence the task entrusted to us as Christians would be impossible if we were not partakers of the first fruits of the Spirit. Therefore, in the second section Paul speaks not only of the actions of the Spirit in the world but of his action among Christians, in the Church. He or she is a Christian who has realized Jesus Christ as the great gift of God, as the gift of a new freedom, of an all-surpassing fulfillment in faith; he or she is a Christian who through baptism shares in the Spirit of Jesus Christ. The mystery of God is made visible in Jesus Christ. Therefore, Jesus Christ is our decisive standard for the discernment of spirits. At the same time he is our pledge that the action of the Spirit has broken through in history; that a new beginning has been established: one that continues to take effect through the Spirit in the Church.

Here we must pause. Do we really sense any evidence of the Holy Spirit in the Church? Surely in the Church too there is much uncertainty, argument, lack of courage, much fear and resignation, and sometimes also much evidence of an unholy spirit. On this account many people are annoyed or scandalized by the Church and take offense at its inadequacies and errors. Paul does not try to argue his way out of such negative aspects of the Church. In fact he is not sparing of his criticism of them. That is why he speaks of the groaning of the Spirit in Christians. He knows that they carry their riches in earthen vessels. There is no trace of self-satisfied triumphalism in Paul. If the Holy Spirit were to be so unambiguously identified and defined, then he would not be the Holy Spirit himself but our own small spirit. Hence in the Church, too, the Holy Spirit can only be perceived through confrontations, and in the suffering of and persistence through conflicts. If we could see hope it would not be hope itself.

Nevertheless, Paul in his epistles tells of many signs of the action of the Spirit in the Church. He is constantly encouraged and strengthened in his apostolic endeavors because he finds other people who believe, because he comes across to colleagues, and because he discovers communities that support him in his work. For Paul the experience of the Spirit is a communal affair. Today, too, aided by Jesus Christ and his Spirit, people accept and affirm one another; give one another courage and hope; help one another in a spirit of fellowship in word and deed; come together and thus enable one another to learn something of the joy of being Christians; assemble to celebrate the eucharist, and thereby become aware that they cannot decide their lives for themselves but owe their fulfillment to the Spirit of God. We must remember what would really be missing in our society and in our lives if there were no Church, and if our parish or community did not exist. Think of the words of encouragement, the *diaconia* of love, the celebration of God's mystery that would be missing from our lives.

No one can objectively demonstrate such experiences. One has to live them oneself in order to relate them to others, to bear witness and invite others to try as well. Hence Pentecost is an invitation to being in the Church, to existence in the Christian community. It is not an invitation to be in a Church from which, quite passively, one awaits some service, but a request to be in a Church in which one actively is oneself, which one lives, and which one responsibly forms. Often in history this Church has been placed under sentence of death, and yet ever and again it has shown an astonishing ability to live on. Whoever lives in and with the Church learns that today, too, there is much more that is alive and kicking in it than can possibly be seen from outside. Whoever entrusts himself or herself to the Church can enter into a wholly new world, and experience that he or she is not lonely and alone, but that there is something beyond the usual superficial encounters; that he or she is accepted and supported by the Holy Spirit in all profundity, and accepted and supported by a greater "we" — the Christian community which lives in the spirit of hope and is scattered throughout all nations.

3. The Spirit in the life of the individual

Paul sees the Spirit not only in the world and not only in the Church. The Spirit takes effect in every baptized person. According to Paul every baptized person has his or her gift of the Spirit. Here we touch on the most profound mystery of Christian life. But many people would take these statements as purely mythological and ideological and ask: Where in my personal life can I learn something of the Spirit of God? Where is his action audible?

Experience of the Spirit

We would certainly misunderstand Paul if we thought that he was speaking only of isolated, specifically gifted Christians. There *is* something that we might call the mysticism of everyday Christian life. Everyone who does not live superficially but is alive to the profound nature of his or her existence, experiences something of the mystery of his or her life that is not capable of being conceptualized. Such people sense in their consciences something of an inner striving toward the good and of warning about what is evil. Many ignore such signs. They are so busy with their plans, following their own interests and looking to their own advantage, that they have neither room nor time for anything else. Other people try to secure themselves and shut themselves off from the disturbing mystery of their lives. They prefer even a solitary path to the broad way which others take. But it can also happen that someone suddenly ignores all the usual reservations and, though it seems tactically stupid and unprofitable, trust in another person in spite of frequent deceptions. Such people commit themselves courageously and wholeheartedly to some major concern, even though the prospects of success are probably not very rosy. They do not despair in a tough situation but see it out bravely and patiently. Anyone who is prepared in this way to abandon generally acceptable norms, and even self, can experience something of the freely creative power of the Spirit of Jesus Christ.

But you will ask whence the power and courage to achieve such freedom come.... Paul replies that the Spirit comes to the aid of our weakness in teaching us to pray: "Abba, Father." The experience of prayer is the most profound form of experience of the Spirit. No fine, impressive words are needed. Paul speaks of a mute form of travail. It is an open question whether by that he means ecstatic discourse or a simple "Thou" to God as the ultimate and deepest mystery. In any event he is concerned with the experience of an ultimate certainty, a basic trust that overcomes all anxieties of existence because it knows that it is absolutely accepted and hidden in God. One cannot "make" such experiences, but one can make a peaceful space for oneself in order to be open and prepared for them. If such experiences are then entrusted to one they can completely change life; they can heal and sanctify. Without such profound transformations our being a Christian becomes a soul-less form of action; but if they happen there is true renewal in the Church and in society. Therefore, the practice of prayer and prayer-experiences are decisive factors in determining whether our Christian life is a living thing or a pious but ossified, empty, and soul-less pursuit.

And so there are experiences of the Spirit — in the world, in the Church and in our life as an individual. Finally, all that remains is to adress this same Spirit in the words of an old hymn:

> Come, Holy Ghost; Creator, come,
> inspire the souls of thine;
> Till every heart which thou hast made
> is filled with grace divine.
> Thou art the Comforter, the gift
> of God, and fire of love;
> The everlasting spring of Joy,
> and unction from above.
> Thy gifts are manifold, thou wrt'st
> God's laws in each true heart;
> The promise of the Father, thou
> dost heavenly speech impart.

Experience of the Spirit

Enlighten our dark souls, till they
thy sacred love embrace;
Assist our mind, by nature frail,
with thy celestial grace.
Drive far from us the mortal foe,
and give us peace within;
That, by thy guidance blessed, we may
escape the snares of sin.
Teach us the Father to confess,
and Son, from death revived;
And, with them both, the Holy Ghost,
Who art from both derived.
With thee, O Father, therefore, may
the Son, from death restored,
And sacred Comforter, one God,
devoutly be adored:
As in all ages heretofore
Has constantly been done,
As now it is, and shall be so
When time his course has run.

IX
Bread for the Life of the World
Corpus Christi: Luke 9:10-17

"BREAD FOR THE life of the world." These words summarize the Gospel for Corpus Christi. They are very relevant now. For our world is hungry. Hungry in many different ways. For bread, for meaning, for God. Hunger is one of the signs of our times.

1. Daily Bread

More than two-thirds of mankind are without their daily bread. Most of them have no home that is worthy of a human being, and many have no work. When we come together as Christians to celebrate our holy meal we cannot ignore this. The God whom we celebrate is a God of mankind. In the Old Testament we read how God miraculously fed his people on their way through the wilderness. The New Testament Gospel for Corpus Christi refers to that account. Jesus does not feed people with pious words but with their daily bread. Part of Jesus' message of the coming kingdom of God is the feeding of the masses, eating meals with the rejected of those days — the sinners, tax collectors, prostitutes — and the healing of the sick. Jesus uses signs to foretell what will come in all fullness in the kingdom of God. All tears will be wiped away; all suffering will be removed; and there will be justice and peace for ever for all nations.

When we come together on Corpus Christi in the name of Jesus to celebrate our meal in public, then we do so in order to bear festive witness to that hope. Therefore, the eucharist is not only the private affair of each individual present. And it is not the esoteric concern of a group of pious people. It is a public sign, a sign of hope. Hence it is a contradiction of the comfortable opinion that the world must always be as it is and that it can never change. A fatalism fixed in the present is not only dangerous but contrary to the Gospel; it is un-Christian. Corpus Christi is a demonstration of hope in a new humanity, in a kingdom of peace and justice, and in a world of neighborliness and sharing. The celebration of the eucharist is an appeal to our social conscience and to our public responsibility. We have to ask ourselves whether we have not compromised ourselves as Christians and trimmed ourselves with the times; and whether we have not anxiously hidden the fire of hope and become fundamentally and terribly lacking in any expectation. Hope in the kingdom of God must make us uneasy in a world full of hunger.

2. The bread of the word

Man does not live by bread alone. He is hungry for more: for love, for acceptance, for reconciliation and for meaning in his life. Nowadays we are not only plagued by bodily need, by care for our daily bread. Albert Einstein once said that in earlier times people had perfect goals but imperfect means to achieve them. Today we have almost perfect means which allow us to achieve almost everything but only quite confused goals. Our deepest need is our spiritual poverty, our spiritual confusion and lack of orientation. What we need and what the world needs from us is therefore not our daily bread but the bread of the word of God. Today, more than ever perhaps, it is bread for the life of the world.

Our eucharistic celebration begins with a service of the word. The renewal of the service of the word is one of the great gifts of the conciliar renewal. Yet it is of little value if we read the gospel merely in celebration, as it were. It has to enter into us and inspire us. We must listen to it as a form of critical inquiry into our lives, and we must be ready to set our standards by it — which means we have to convert and to believe. Corpus Christi is an appeal to consider the very basis and direction of our lives. Whence do we live? By what *people* say, do and think, or by what God says to us? There is nothing more important than the bread of the word that gives our lives support and content and meaning and mission, so that we can hear, read, consider, and give forth.

3. The eucharistic bread

The daily bread and the bread of the word of God are not the ultimate food. God wants the whole man. He is not only present through his word. He is also present in living signs. In the celebration of the eucharist his word takes on living form in the bread and wine. The whole way in which Jesus, according to today's Gospel, distributed the bread to the people shows that the evangelist was not thinking of any ordinary meal. Before Jesus distributes the food he looks up to the Father, prays over the bread and blesses it. Feeding with our daily bread and the eucharistic meal are one here. Hence the feeding of the five thousand anticipates the meal that Jesus shared with the twelve on the night before his death, when he gave himself to his disciples in the sign of a meal. Jesus' great bequest to us is that he himself wishes to remain among us as our life. It is he who brings us together on this day and invites us so that he can eat with us. Here is the essential mystery of this feast, a mystery that no man can solve, a mystery that we can only approach in reverence.

Therefore, we must pause a moment in order to consider what is meant by the foregoing. The liturgical renewal of the last few decades has shown us anew the meaning of eucharistic celebration. The rites have been altered and have become comprehensible. The language of the people has replaced Latin so that everyone can really take part in the celebration. There is still much to be done to make services more lively and spontaneous, and to ensure that joy is not dampened. External reforms cannot do that. The profound meaning of the eucharist is something that we shall only understand when we know what people's real hunger and thirst are, and what man's deepest longing is. The Bible says that man is fashioned according to the image and likeness of God. That is why man's heart is so big and his longing so deep that nothing in the world will fulfill them but only God. Our heart will not rest until it rests in You, said one of the greatest of all theologians. Perhaps all the unrest, rush and trouble of our times, the dissatisfaction and the frustration, ultimately show that we lack this deepest fulfillment. But where people are without the basis and goal of their lives, their souls are lost. Being without God is the real lack of our times. It makes our lives empty and banal.

The real service that the Church can perform for people today is therefore to celebrate divine service. All our lives will become more human if we once again see divine service as the center of our existence. The eucharist is bread for the life of the world, bread for our own lives.

For us Corpus Christi is not just a feast. It is so to speak a prism comprising the whole of our faith and hope — hope in the coming of the kingdom of God in which there will be no need and universal peace will reign. Through the word of God and the bread of life this new world enters into our own world, in order to give our lives direction and power. In word and sacrament God is already among us in a hidden form. Corpus Christi is an answer to the hunger and need of our age. "Therefore," we sing, "let us honor this great Sacrament. This covenant will last forever and the old form has come to an end."

What we celebrate in Corpus Christi is the hidden beginning of a fulfillment which exceeds all hunger and all longing. Therefore, let us give thanks and celebrate the eucharist. It is meet and right so to do.